SUMMARY

&ANALYSIS

OF

ENLIGHTENMENT NOW

THE CASE FOR REASON, SCIENCE, HUMANISM, AND PROGRESS

A GUIDE TO THE BOOK
BY STEVEN PINKER

BY **ZIP**READS

TABLE OF CONTENTS

Key Takeaway: The environment is better off than it was in 1970.
Key Takeaway: Carbon accumulation and climate change are the biggest threats to humanity in existence.

Peace
Key Takeaway: There are fewer wars, and fewer people are dying in current wars, than at any time in history.

Safety
Key Takeaway: Violent crime is lower than it ever has been in history.
Key Takeaway: With the sole exception of drug overdoses, every type of accidental death has significantly declined.

Terrorism
Key Takeaway: Terrorism is not the danger that most Americans perceive it to be.
Key Takeaway: Right-wing extremists kill more Americans than Islamic terrorists.

Democracy
Key Takeaway: The world has become more democratic over time, though not at a steady pace

Equal Rights
Key Takeaway: Discrimination, prejudice, and hate crimes are all decreasing.
Key Takeaway: The worldwide movement towards egalitarianism is driven by modernization.

Reason
Key Takeaway: Politicization is the greatest enemy of reason facing the world today.
Key Takeaway: For reason to prevail, we must depoliticize the conversation.

Science
Key Takeaway: Science has been the scapegoat for many crimes against humanity throughout history.
Key Takeaway: Science, religion, art, culture, history, philosophy, and morality are all inextricably intertwined.
Key Takeaway: Liberal arts and the humanities need science in order to remain relevant in the Age of Information.

Humanism
Key Takeaway: Humanism is the best basis for government, society, law, and morality that humans have come up with.

SYNOPSIS

In his book *Enlightenment Now,* Steven Pinker makes the case that the Enlightenment ideals of sympathy and reason are both valuable and necessary tools to help humanity *flourish*. Despite the doom and gloom dominating the news cycles of late, Pinker posits that humanity is much better off than they ever have been before—and he has the data to prove it.

Using the four tenets of the Enlightenment: reason, science, humanism, and progress, Pinker aims to paint these 17th, 18th and 19th century ideals with a modern brush and argues that humanism is the only reasonable system of belief by which a modern world should be governed. Utilizing modern language, modern concepts, modern science, and modern technology, he illustrates in almost tedious detail just how far humanity has come since the first Enlightenment was upon us, and how humanism has been the necessary, driving force behind that advancement.

Throughout the book, Pinker systematically addresses every aspect of personal well-being there is: from health and wealth to safety and culture, as well as measures of societal well-being such as human rights, inequality, and the environment. No stone is left unturned in his exhaustive, comparative examination of life in every country around the world from the Middle Ages to present day.

For each argument he presents, Pinker offers common fallacies, counter-arguments, and pitfalls of leaders, thinkers, and intellectuals from both the right and left side of the political spectrum.

Enlightenment Now is painstakingly researched with dozens of graphics and charts and over 70 pages of notes and references to support his near innumerable claims about where humanity has been, where we are, and where we're headed next.

PART I: ENLIGHTENMENT

CHAPTER 1

In order to understand the Enlightenment, there are four basic ideals one must understand: reason, science, humanism, and progress.

Reason

One of most distinctive differences of the Enlightenment as compared to the preceding period of history is the value of reason. Striving for reason means tossing aside the delusional effects of things like dogma, authority, and mysticism. It was reason that led most thinkers to question the existence of an unquestionable God and to begin to see alternative possibilities for how the world is organized and may have come to be.

"The deliberate application of reason was necessary precisely because our common habits of thought were not particularly reasonable" (Pinker, p. 8).

Science

The number of discoveries since the dawn of the Scientific Revolution that we now take for granted as common knowledge is astounding—that the Earth revolves around the Sun, that the Earth is not flat, that werewolves and witches aren't real—to name a few. Beyond the supernatural and superstitious, science opened a door for humanity that changed the world from a frightening place to an understandable one. Lightning bolts, droughts, comets, eclipses and other previously inexplicable phenomena, most frequently attributed to benevolent or malicious higher powers, could now be seen without the fear and paranoia that previously defined them. Science is the natural extension of reason; it is the tool through which reason is applied and verified.

Humanism

After centuries of religious carnage including the Crusades, the Inquisition, and the Salem witch trials, Enlightenment thinkers saw an "urgent need for a secular foundation for morality" (Pinker, p.10). One of the key tenets of the new humanistic morality was the concept that the individual is held above the group. Humanism requires the understanding that each and every human on the planet has the exact same capacity to *flourish* and to suffer, and that we have no choice but to recognize and respect that. Much of modern law and democracy are built upon similar ideals: you are free to pursue your own happiness so long as it doesn't impede on another man's pursuit of his.

Humanism is embodied by the innate capacity for sympathy that all humans share. In the context of the Enlightenment, that capacity meant the theoretical end of barbaric practices that were previously commonplace such as slavery and torture. According to Pinker, it extends to many more practices throughout history and the future.

Progress

The final of the original Enlightenment ideals is perhaps one most modern people take for granted: progress. It is critical, however, not to confuse progress in urban development or technological convenience as real progress. He argues that, "progress unguided by humanism is not progress" (Pinker, p. 11).

As such, progress must be seen as any development which makes the lives of humanity better as a whole, which allows us to *flourish*. The progress of societies is anything that provides more freedom, structure, or opportunity to this end. Governments, schools, laws, markets, and international bodies that are created for this purpose (or function with this goal in mind) all represent progress from the perspective of the Enlightenment. A change in regulation that would benefit the super wealthy at the expense of the middle class, or a shift in international policy that favors nationalism and reduces aid to the poor, would not.

CHAPTER 2

Pinker asserts that any modern iteration of the Enlightenment must be amended to include advancements and discoveries that have been made since that time. The three he offers are "Entro, Evo, Info."

Entropy

In a closed system, entropy never decreases. This is the Second Law of Thermodynamics and, according to Pinker, is applicable far beyond a physics laboratory.

Entropy is disorder. All things will tend towards disorder unless they are otherwise acted upon to restore that order. Pinker frames this concept by having the reader imagine a sand castle. Will the same sand castle be there tomorrow? Of course not, because there is an infinitely higher number of ways for the sand to NOT be a castle than to be one.

As humans, our concept of order and of things being "right" is highly limited. As such, the state of disorder is basically every other option except the one we believe to be correct and pleasing. The constant movement of the world into disorder forces us to react to keep it in place; we clean our kitchens so the dishes don't pile up, and we tend to our relationships lest they fall apart. We are constantly working towards order in a world that is moving in the opposite direction.

Evolution

With the understanding of evolution, the scientific community transitioned from seeing the elegance of the human body as evidence of a divine power to understanding it as a series of accidental mutations that had no choice but to lead to improvements. It may seem in itself that evolution is proof of order in a system: organisms become more efficient over time. But Pinker counters this by pointing out that we as organisms are not a closed system. We require energy from external sources to fight that entropy, and those energies we consume affect our development, our very cellular structure.

The consumption of energy is the necessary and basic fighting force against entropy and is present in all living things. There is no evolution without energy; there is no progress without energy; there is no progress without evolution.

Information

"Information may be thought of as a reduction in entropy—as the ingredient that distinguishes an orderly, structured system from the vast set of random, useless ones" (Pinker, pp. 19–20).

Information has always been powerful, but never before have we had such power over information. With the dawn of technology, of computers, of data analysis, we are able to understand more about our systems—both biological and machine—and how to harness the energy we create. We can use information in order to fight the entropy that threatens us constantly. A growing wealth of human knowledge gave us the power to cook food, to farm food, to drill for oil to make energy, and to make the great escape from widespread poverty.

Information gives us the freedom to transcend our physical needs and focus on spiritual, ethical, and human needs. We use energy to organize information to fight the entropy of the system and to progress. This theme recurs throughout the book on a scale from micro to macro. The increase in access to information means an increased ability for humans to flourish. And *flourishing* is the ultimate goal of an Enlightenment agenda.

CHAPTER 3

Counter-Enlightenments

The recent rising tide of populism, nationalism, authoritarianism, and fundamental religion are just a few examples Pinker offers of forces fighting back against Enlightenment thinking.

He is careful to mention that these "counter-enlightenments" aren't just coming from the right of the political spectrum. Plenty of left-wing activists and intellectuals are willing to forgo individual rights for the higher causes of racial and gender equality, or to sacrifice our own need to create energy (and fight entropy) in order to "save" the environment. Many intellectuals are anti-science, lack reason, and have lost sight of the bigger picture behind the causes they're fighting for.

Above all, left-wing and right-wing ideologies have themselves become dogmas. Voting for president is more akin to rooting for your team to win the big game than considering a candidate's position on an issue or engaging in civil discourse.

Pinker uses this chapter to set up the naysayers of Enlightenment thought, which he will spend the rest of the book arguing against.

PART II: PROGRESS

CHAPTER 4

Progressophobia

Progressophobia is the refusal of most people to accept that the world is getting better despite evidence to the contrary. Pessimism is in fashion among intellectuals and believing that things are good or getting better is often seen as a false, comforting, idealistic, and rosy-colored view of the world. The only problem with this is that things *are* getting better, and no one seems to want to admit it.

Pinker offers several explanations for this:

In a phenomenon known as *the optimism gap*, people are more likely to believe their own lives are likely to get better, while simultaneously believing society as a whole will get worse.

The Availability heuristic refers to the irrational effect that the more often we see something, the more common it is. As news channels are filled with terrorist attacks, plane crashes, and tornadoes, we believe these are more common ways to die than car accidents and asthma attacks (not by a long shot).

Negativity Bias states that even when two things are of equal intensity, things of a more negative nature will have a stronger effect on one's psychological state than neutral or positive events. We suffer losses harder than we celebrate wins, and we are more hurt by criticism than uplifted by praise. Even if the news were reporting the exact same proportion of positive and negative news, we would still be inclined to think things are getting worse.

How do we fight these irrational tendencies? Data.

"A quantitative mindset, despite its nerdy aura, is in fact the morally enlightened one, because it treats every human life as having equal value rather than privileging the people who are closest to us or most photogenic" (Pinker, p. 43).

CHAPTER 5

Life

In this chapter, Pinker provides extensive data that life is longer. He does not argue whether it is better or more fulfilling, just that it is longer, that it continues to get longer, and that this is true for everyone in the world.

Key Takeaway: Life expectancy has increased dramatically in every country in the past 50 years.

- In the mid-18th century, life expectancy in Europe and the Americas was around 35 years. In 2015, that number was over 71.4 for the entire world and over 81 for the most developed nations.

- Every country in the world has a lower rate of child mortality today than in 1950.

- The rate at which mothers die in childbirth has dropped precipitously since the early 20th century.

- Even the poorest populations in the world have experienced significant improvements in health and longevity.

CHAPTER 6

Health

Key Takeaway: Even basic improvements in the understanding of science and health have saved billions of human lives.

Since the beginning of time, humanity has been plagued by incurable disease. While early *Homo sapiens* may have tried such outdated techniques as bloodletting and animal sacrifice, from the late 18th century onward we have witnessed vast improvements in the understanding and treatment of disease.

Among others, this includes discoveries such as vaccination, penicillin, antisepsis, anesthesia, and a general scientific understanding and acceptance of what germs are and how they work.

Beyond the complicated and often expensive procedures in modern medicine that have saved hundreds of millions of lives in the 20th century alone, what has arguably saved even more is basic knowledge of sanitation: boiling water before you drink it, washing your hands regularly, and defecating in toilets or latrines.

CHAPTER 7

Sustenance

Improvements in farming practices, selective breeding of higher performing crops, and vast leaps in agricultural technology have led to a food supply trending far upward of early predictions while prices have dropped dramatically.

Key Takeaway: The world is producing enough food for the entire world to eat.

Since the 1980s, deaths from famine around the world have decreased dramatically, and famine appears to have been all but eradicated in the 21st century with a few exceptions on the African continent.

There is an increase in available calories per capita across the spectrum from rich to poor and in both developed and underdeveloped countries.

Undernourishment—a year or more of insufficient food—is also trending downward in developing countries, while remaining stable for the fully developed countries such as the United States.

Key Takeaway: There is no such thing as a non-GMO crop.

Intellectual environmental purists decry the benefits of genetically superior, modified crops as "unnatural" and "dangerous" when in reality, there is no such thing as a non-GMO crop. Every crop that we eat—from wheat to corn to carrots—is drastically different today than it was a hundred years ago due to genetic mutations manipulated by farmers. The process is just much faster and more efficient today.

Key Takeaway: Famine is not caused solely by drought, flood, and poverty.

Believing that famine is a natural disaster is a red herring. Modern famine is more often triggered by war, civil unrest, Communist collectivization, callous governments, colonization, import restrictions, and many other man-made calamities.

CHAPTER 8

Wealth

Pinker commonly refers to "The Great Escape," a term coined by economist, Angus Deaton for humanity's release from poverty, famine, and premature death. This escape is inarguably linked to the vast creation of wealth around the world.

When talking about comparative wealth, we often speak in terms like "in 1820 dollars" or "adjusted for inflation," but more important than an equal evaluation of the worth of a dollar in the year 2000 or the year 1820 is what items were *available* to buy. How much richer is a lower-middle-class person in the 21st century who owns a computer, a tablet, a refrigerator, and has central A/C and heating than an aristocrat in the 18th century who had vast wealth, but could have none of those things? How do you quantify that difference?

Key Takeaway: Wealth is not finite, it is created.

From the year 0 to the year 1820, the world essentially saw no growth in wealth. A chart depicting such growth looks more like a flat line than a graph. But then, between 1820 and 1900, the world's income tripled. Then it tripled again in under 50 years, then 25 years, then 33 years, tripling again each time. This equates to growth of over a hundredfold since 1820. The chart from 1820 to the year 2000 looks like a 90-degree angle upwards. In other words: almost all of the wealth in the entire world didn't exist 100 years ago. And more is *created* every day.

Key Takeaway: There are three main drivers of wealth creation in human history: science, institutions, and a change in values.

Without the science and technology to improve existing products and create new ones, as well as to increase productivity, it is easy to see how an economy wouldn't grow.

Without institutions such as banks and governments and laws, the exchange of goods can be a difficult and suspicious process. How can I trust that your product is good, or your gold is real? Institutions provide the safety net for positive-sum commerce to take place.

But the real driver is the change in social values. Commerce was once something for the poor, lower classes as the aristocracy had no need for it. Sometime in the 18th century, commerce itself came to be viewed as an ideal marker of success in a society.

Key Takeaway: In the late 20th century, the Great Escape spread, rising poor countries out of poverty—referred to as "The Great Convergence."

"Since 1995, 30 of the world's 109 developing countries … have enjoyed economic growth rates that amount to a doubling of income every eighteen years" (Pinker, pp. 85–86).

Despite the growth in inequality in Western industrialized countries, the world as a whole is getting richer and more equal.

The five main contributors to the Great Convergence are:

· The decline of communism and collectivist economies

· A change in leadership in developing countries

- The end of the Cold War

- Globalization

- Science and technology

Key Takeaway: Higher GDP correlates with "every indicator of human flourishing."

These indicators include the obvious such as health, longevity, and nutrition, but also softer indicators like peace, freedom, human rights and tolerance. Richer countries are also happier, smarter, have fewer wars, have more participatory democracies, and a wealth of other positive changes.

CHAPTER 9

Inequality

According to Pinker, the left's new uproar over and obsession with rising income equality isn't wrong—income inequality is rising in many Western nations—but the ire is misguided.

Morally speaking, it shouldn't matter if someone has more than you, so long as you both have enough. While this may be true from an objective standpoint, social comparison theory means that we as humans may *feel* poorer than we are, and therefore less happy, when compared to someone with so much more than we have.

From this, one would conclude (and the left often argues) that people in the countries with the highest levels of inequality (such as Brazil and South Africa) should be the least happy people. A lower-middle-class person in America should be less happy than a poverty-stricken person in Communist Chechnya—because everyone there is equally poor. The data according to Pinker do not agree.

Key Takeaway: Living in a poor country with less inequality still equates to *less* happiness than a rich country with high inequality

In addition to inequality not causing unhappiness, inequality caused by growing and progressing economies drives its own equalizing force: social spending. The larger a country's economy grows, the larger percent of GDP they will spend on social welfare programs, which uplift the poorest subsection of any population, and in turn further increase happiness levels of the population as a whole.

Key Takeaway: Inequality may be rising within highly developed countries, but is decreasing in the world as a whole, as is poverty across the board.

On a relative scale, the biggest losers to inequality in the entire world are the lower middle classes of the wealthiest countries. They have seen the smallest gains relative to the very rich and the very poor. While this explains so much of the anger from those white, factory-working, marginalized

Americans, the message is clear: if everyone is less poor than they used to be, it can't be a bad thing.

Even those who are the "worst off" are far and away objectively better than they have been at any time before.

"The old stereotype of poverty was an emaciated pauper in rags. Today, the poor are likely to be as overweight as their employers, and dressed in the same fleece, sneakers, and jeans" (Pinker, p. 117).

There are fewer poor people in the world. There are fewer poor people in developed countries. The people who are poor are less poor than they used to be. Pinker effectively disproves that popular mantra—the rich *are* getting richer, but the poor are not getting poorer.

CHAPTER 10

The Environment

Ecomodernism is a new approach to environmentalism that abandons the romanticism of the green movement that began in the 1970s and offers a new practicality to the concept. Pinker argues that many far-left environmentalists today view the problem as a linear issue—a one-way train headed for critical mass destruction—when the reality is that human ingenuity has already avoided every previously predicted pitfall, and it is likely we will continue to do so. At the same time, the political right denies environmental issues even exist, which is an equally troubling stance.

People have always harmed the environment and created entropy and waste, long before the Industrial Revolution. Industrialization has also been very good for humanity. Any detriment to the planet must be weighed against the benefits of electricity, warmth, comfort, and prosperity.

Key Takeaway: Doomsday prophecies of overpopulation and resource scarcity are a myth.

Time and again humanity has been warned of the exponential curve of the population graph. Liberal intellectuals especially have been offering draconian predictions on overpopulation since the 1950s. The reality is that population growth naturally declines as wealth increases. Fertility rates around the world are dropping as women marry later and have fewer children. Data suggests that world population will hit its peak sometime around 2070 and then begin to decline.

Resource scarcity as well has been threatened in the 20th century for everything from oil to water to rare minerals. A supply and demand economy dictates that rare materials are more expensive, are used more carefully, and technology is constantly being created to replace that which is no longer viable. Humans have never run out of a material we couldn't replace with something better.

Key Takeaway: The environment is better off than it was in 1970.

The effects of the creation of the EPA on the environment are incontrovertible. Despite an increase in population, vehicles owned, and miles driven, we are producing significantly lower emissions and are increasingly energy efficient. Smog is lower, water is cleaner, deforestation is down, as are oil spills. The reason for this is we are using less to do more.

Dematerialization, or the use of fewer materials to yield the same outcome, means we continue to consume less across all areas of our lives. From the digital revolution to the sharing economy, we just don't have as much *stuff*. And the stuff we do produce and consume is many times more efficient in its use of materials than initial iterations.

Key Takeaway: Carbon accumulation and climate change are the biggest threats to humanity in existence.

Pinker warns in unequivocal terms that carbon accumulation and climate change are the biggest threats to humanity, but that only an enlightened environmental approach can solve them. He cautions against the illogical and counter-productive actions of the far-left environmentalists as equally as he does against the regulation rollback of the Trump administration.

While he presents a variety of potential solutions, including a strong call for transition back to nuclear power as well as the possibility of large-scale "climate engineering" to lower the Earth's temperature, the core of his argument lies in the fact that we must USE energy to fight the entropy of the system. The problem of carbon emissions can only be solved through an enlightened approach. Problems are solvable, but that does not mean they solve themselves (Pinker, p. 155).

CHAPTER 11

Peace

Key Takeaway: There are fewer wars, and fewer people are dying in current wars, than at any time in history.

Despite your own availability bias and what you see on the news, far less of the world is at war—and far fewer people are dying from war—than at any time since the end of WWII.

Democratic nations are less likely to go to war with one another than authoritarian nations, and we have many more democratic nations since the end of the Cold War. One of the biggest reasons the number of wars has declined, however, is simply because we made war *illegal*. Since the formation of the United Nations in 1945 there has been a real and measurable punishment for anyone who breaks this international law.

While Pinker readily admits that a decline in world wars can change at any time, he warns specifically of the rise of nationalism and populism as precursors to the Great Wars of the past.

CHAPTER 12

Safety

"Accidents are the fourth-leading cause of death in the United States, after heart disease, cancer, and respiratory diseases" (Pinker, p. 167).

In this chapter, Pinker examines the multitude of ways that humans can die outside of natural causes. Covering everything from homicide rates to poison ingestion, he concludes that advancements in safety are an unsung success of the Enlightenment. He also states with categorial certainty that we are living in the safest time in history.

Pinker is clear to thwart any naysayers of modernity by confirming that none of our technological advances have made us any less safe than before they were invented. Medieval Europe had a particularly hilarious and gruesome collection of ways to die that seem utterly ridiculous to a modern person, and you were more likely to die by a horse-drawn carriage trampling you than you are in a motor vehicle today.

Key Takeaway: Violent crime is lower than it ever has been in history.

Beginning with the Civilizing Process of the 14th century—the transition to resolving disputes in less violent ways—a reduction in violent crime was further fueled by a worldwide movement towards centralized governments and positive-sum systems of commerce. Frequently referencing his own book on violent crime, *The Better Angels of Our Nature,* Pinker shows in no uncertain terms that rates of violent crime are lower than at any time in history, no matter what the news and your Availability bias would have you believe.

Even in countries with extremely high homicide rates, the violence is highly localized—not just in countries, but in specific cities in those countries, in specific neighborhoods in those cities, and often by specific people.

Key Takeaway: With the sole exception of drug overdoses, every type of accidental death has significantly declined.

Car, pedestrian, and airline deaths, and even deaths from falling, drowning, and fires have precipitously dropped since the early 20th century. Thanks to increased safety measures, regulations, and the sheer power of data analysis, workplace accidents have gone from a daily reality of risky industrial careers to a mostly preventable, though still unfortunate, anomaly. Many of these safety measures in our cars, our homes, and our jobs were not just implemented in response to some specific legislation, but occurred naturally as humans figured out better, safer, more efficient ways of doing things. Others were propelled forward by activists, watchdog groups, and concerned citizens. The wealthier a country, the safer they became, irrespective of regulation.

In this, Pinker sees the Enlightenment ideal of 'progress with humanism at heart' truly shine. These advancements didn't always make things cheaper, faster, or easier, but they preserved human life, which is of the utmost value. Though humans are still dumb enough to put their hands into fires, jump off buildings, and swallow laundry detergent, they are now far less likely to die from doing it.

CHAPTER 13

Terrorism

Unsurprisingly, Pinker's take on terrorism is that the consensus of fear and imminent danger is incorrect, and that terrorism does not pose a real threat to our government, our system, our way of life, or even most of our citizens. By first illustrating how few people terrorism kills in Western countries, and then explaining how ineffective terrorism is at achieving its goals on a larger scale, Pinker effectively snuffs any conversation that terrorism is a force to be reckoned with. On the contrary—the rise of terrorism in the news media is actually a sign that our country is *more* safe, not less, as we have fewer large scale wars to consume our time, energy, and fear as we have in history.

Key Takeaway: Terrorism is not the danger that most Americans perceive it to be.

If you are American, you are hundreds of times more likely to die from homicide than a terror attack, twice as likely to die in a car accident than to be murdered, and almost five times as likely to die from any other kind of accident as a car accident. In sum, you are about 3,000 times more likely to die from a random accident (like drowning in the bathtub or having a refrigerator fall on you) than you are from a terrorist attack.

Key Takeaway: Right-wing extremists kill more Americans than Islamic terrorists.

Though hard to swallow, if you exclude the 9/11 attacks and the Oklahoma City bombing, right-wing extremists have killed TWICE as many people as Islamic terrorists on American soil.

CHAPTER 14

Democracy

"Chaos is deadlier than tyranny" (Pinker, p. 199).

There is no shortage of books being released today proclaiming the end of democracy as we know it and the rise of authoritarianism, dictatorships, and fascism. While these movements are certainly growing and gaining hold in certain countries, worldwide democracy continues to be on the rise—albeit at an unsteady pace. The appeal of democracy is simple: it provides the populace a balance between safety from the violence of anarchy and safety from the violence of tyranny. Too little government, and people kill each other. Too much government, and the government kills the people. The benefits of democracy from a humanistic point of view include higher economic growth, fewer wars and genocides, healthier and better-educated citizens, and virtually no famines. From all accounts, democracy has helped humanity to *flourish*, and therefore is the preferred government for an Enlightenment thinker.

Key Takeaway: The world has become more democratic over time, though not at a steady pace

Though defining democracy can be an exercise in grey areas, there is no question that more countries are becoming full democracies, and more countries are becoming more democratic (while technically remaining under a dictatorship, for example). China, though still under authoritarian rule has far more personal freedoms and civil liberties than they have in the past. In 2015, there were 103 democracies in the world, compared to just 52 in 1989. Two-thirds of the world's population is now living in a free or relatively free society.

While the trend towards democracy ebbs and flows with political trends, there is no doubt, according to Pinker, that it is the best form of government the planet has come up with so far.

CHAPTER 15

Equal Rights

Once again, Pinker presents a chapter flooded with optimism showing the reader that all signs point to *flourish*. Here we find less discrimination, universal women's suffrage (save for Vatican City), a decrease in child labor, and an increase in "emancipative values" on a worldwide basis. Even in the most conservative countries in the Middle East where these values are comparatively low, they are still on the rise.

Key Takeaway: Discrimination, prejudice, and hate crimes are all decreasing.

According to search data obtained from Google searches, public discrimination isn't just down, but people's private perception of prejudice is down as well. People are not only not *acting* racist, they don't *feel* racist. This trend also applies to homophobia and sexism. Society is becoming more tolerant and that tolerance increases with each new generation.

Key Takeaway: The worldwide movement towards egalitarianism is driven by modernization.

Citing Maslow's hierarchy of needs, humans need to first tend to their physiological needs (food, shelter and safety) before they can turn to their emotional needs (belonging and esteem), after which, at the top of the hierarchy, they can find self-actualization. As countries and economies grow, there is no longer a competition for food, shelter, or survival. With this freedom to pursue self-actualization, it seems humans naturally gravitate towards more equality and opportunity for everyone. Pinker refers to these as "emancipative values" and the effect can be seen worldwide.

The largest factor contributing to the upward trend of emancipative values around the world is *knowledge*. The Knowledge Index includes level of education, access to internet, scientific and technological productivity, and institutional integrity. These factors accounted for 70 percent of the differences in emancipative values across countries.

CHAPTER 16

Knowledge

Pinker takes a personal and hopeful tone as he espouses the benefits of education not just on societies, but on individuals in those societies and the enrichment it can have on their personal lives. Higher levels of education lead to economic growth, and economic growth is at the same time a boon to education. Education and knowledge are flagships of human progress, and no enlightened society is complete without them. Most notably in the progression of history is the spread of literacy. The last few strongholds of illiteracy in the entire world are three of the poorest and most war-torn countries: South Sudan, the Congo, and Afghanistan. It is predicted that by the end of this century, the worldwide proportion of illiteracy will effectively fall to zero.

Key Takeaway: Intelligence drives GDP growth.

Beyond the worldwide trend towards better education, and gender equality in education, the world is actually getting smarter. Not just more educated, but verifiably smarter. And not just smarter in math and vocabulary, smarter in analytical and abstract thinking. This 30-point increase in IQ scores that can be seen around the world is not just a personal benefit but acts as a predictor of future GDP growth. The higher a country's average IQ, the faster that country's GDP will grow.

While Pinker acknowledges the blur between causation and correlation, he posits that they might not need to be so clearly separated when all of the indicators of human health, success, and happiness are trending in the same direction. If wealth, health, nutrition, education, liberal government and happiness are all on rise, perhaps they are all indefinably intertwined. Pinker argues they are, and we have a name for it: progress.

CHAPTER 17

Quality of Life

"There can be no question of which was the greatest era for culture; the answer has to be today, until it is superseded by tomorrow" (Pinker, p. 261).

With all of the increases in productivity and wealth, many argue that they are being wasted on consumerism, television, and video games, that the American family has fallen apart, that we've lost our core values, and that we're worse off for it. Others believe we're working more than ever before, with no time for leisure or family. Naturally, Pinker, and the data, disagree. In fact, Americans have more leisure time and spend more quality time with their children than they did in the 1960s.

Key Takeaway: There are innumerable, quantifiable factors that have contributed to the increase in quality of life.

- The relative cost of electricity has decreased *twelve thousandfold* since the Middle Ages, meaning more hours are available for humans to read, write, and interact and that those hours cost minute fractions of what they used to

- Kitchen appliances have drastically reduced the amount of time we spend on housework (fighting the entropy of a messy home)

- The proliferation of technology means the ability to keep in touch, to hear, and to see our loved ones at a moment's notice

- We take for granted how recent the entertainment that we have available came to be: as recently as the late 19th century there was no radio, television, movies, or music recordings

CHAPTER 18

Happiness

Despite being objectively better off in basically every way imaginable than we were 100 years ago, if we aren't any happier, what's the point? It's a difficult question to answer on a personal basis (are *you* happy?) and an even more difficult one to quantify.

Measuring happiness means keeping track both of how people feel at a given moment (joy, anger, elation, etc.) as well as how they evaluate their life as a whole (are you satisfied, successful, fulfilled etc.)? In addition to these two dimensions we must include meaning and purpose. All these things considered, are we any happier?

Key Takeaway: The richer the country, the happier the people.

Despite all of the anecdotal evidence about increased depression and malaise and the effect of the Optimism Gap (I'm happy, but everyone else isn't), Pinker's research confirms that an increase in a country's wealth, and therefore their equality, education, and everything else that comes with it, leads to increased happiness. (Note that there are some specific and recent exceptions to this for Americans, which Pinker delves into in detail.)

Key Takeaway: The Age of the Internet has not caused an epidemic of loneliness.

Contrary to sensationalist news and warnings of the social isolation caused by the dominance of social media in daily life, humans are not sadder, lonelier, more depressed, or more suicidal. With a wealth of statistics confirming this around the world, he turns the blame for the perception of the increase on a rise in diagnoses of mental disorders based on a lowering of the bar to qualify. In addition, more "illnesses" have been added to the list "including Avoidant Personality Disorder (which applies to many people who formerly were called shy)" (Pinker, p. 281).

Pinker goes on to argue that this is actually a marker of a more enlightened society: that we are more compassionate and more willing to recognize the struggles of others as legitimate conditions.

Key Takeaway: Increased anxiety may be the sign of a more engaged, progressive society.

While anxiety may show some upticks, especially for American women, Pinker potentially attributes that to the massive rise in personal responsibility that women have undertaken in the last 50 years. Once responsible just for keeping a home, women are now tasked with full-time careers in addition to bearing the lion's share of child rearing. He broadens this stance to apply to all enlightened societies: the more informed we are, the more personally responsible we feel for the future of our planet, and the more active we are in our political systems, the more anxiety we're going to feel. Being a driving force for change isn't easy; having a meaningful life in the long term doesn't always equate to short-term happiness.

CHAPTER 19

Existential Threats

"If the hands of a clock point to a few minutes to midnight for seventy-two years, something is wrong with the clock" (Pinker, p. 311).

Key Takeaway: The end is not nigh.

In listing various world-ending (yet highly unlikely) scenarios—a black hole swallowing the planet; AI enslaving humanity; an asteroid hitting Earth, blacking out the sun and drenching us in corrosive rain—Pinker quickly dismisses them offhand. Likening AI to the mania of Y2K, his tone approaches ridicule of anyone who would be worried about such nonsense.

While he spends slightly more time debunking more credible threats such as biological warfare and cyberterrorism on a nation-state level, the conclusion is the same: none of these things should concern you. And of course, worry and fear-mongering from the media are exacerbating the public's perception of these things.

Key Takeaway: Nuclear proliferation is over and nuclear war is not an imminent threat.

In typically rosy fashion, Pinker doesn't recognize much of an existing threat in nuclear weapons, but he thoroughly investigates every possible situation in which the world could see the detonation of another one. With the continued decommissioning of weapons in both the U.S. and Russia, he argues, it is more likely nuclear weapons disappear altogether than ever get used again.

CHAPTER 20

The Future of Progress

"On what principle is it, that when we see nothing but improvement behind us, we are to expect nothing but deterioration before us?" (Thomas Macaulay, pp. 327-328).

Pinker's unending optimism finally subsides in his opening of the final chapter of Part II. Relaying the statistics he has tirelessly analyzed in the previous nineteen chapters, the reader is suddenly faced with a dire view on the world: 700 million people live in extreme poverty, more than two billion people are oppressed in autocratic states, every year five million people are killed in accidents, and more than 400,000 are murdered (Pinker, p. 325).

These, of course, are the same statistics presented earlier in the book but from a pessimist's point of view. The purpose of this juxtaposition is to illustrate that, despite the immense progress we have witnessed and created, there is still a long way to go.

Key Takeaway: The New Renaissance will be driven not by energy, but by information.

In contrast to the First Machine Age, which was powered by increases in energy production, the second will be fueled by the other anti-entropy force: information. Utilizing the massive power of information that is upon us, this Second Machine Age will bring about advancements that could include everything from curing cancer and Alzheimer's and solving the fossil fuel crisis to transforming global education and eradicating world hunger.

Key Takeaway: Authoritarian populism is the greatest existing threat to the Enlightenment.

Populism, as we've seen on the rise with leaders such as Donald Trump in the United States and Marine Le Pen in France, shifts focus towards the good of the tribe over the flourishing of the individual. In this structure, the needs of the oppressed, minorities, and those less fortunate around the world are neglected in exchange for the betterment of a homogenous group and ire against existing institutions, intellectuals, or the minorities themselves.

Populism, in America specifically, has threatened every aspect of progress covered in this book: fewer Americans have health insurance; protectionist economic policies threaten gains in wealth from globalization; tax reform has exacerbated already widening inequality; environmental regulations have been thoughtlessly stripped away; equal rights have taken blows through anti-Muslim, anti-gay, and anti-Hispanic rhetoric and policy; democracy has been threatened as the freedom of the press is challenged, judicial rulings are ignored, and the president insists upon his ultimate authority; knowledge itself has been rejected by Trump in a "post-factual" world full of baseless claims and wild conspiracy theories; and the existential threat of nuclear war has needlessly been reintroduced as a possible military tactic against North Korea.

Pinker, of course, isn't all doom and gloom. He recognizes (through data) that it's unlikely this populism takes hold in the long run as so much of it is driven by older generations, and the younger Millennials are exceedingly liberal. But he does leave his previously reliable optimism behind in trying to define this sort of staggered progress (two steps forward, one step back), tossing around monikers like "pessimistic hopefulness," "opti-realism," and "radical incrementalism."

PART III: REASON, SCIENCE, AND HUMANISM

CHAPTER 21

Reason

Pinker presents an in-depth defense and analysis of reason—and the threats to it—as it exists in modern society. He does not spend his time attacking dogma, populism, and religious fundamentalism (as those things are already lacking reason) but turns his criticisms towards the intellectuals who embrace Enlightenment philosophy in theory, but often fall short in practice.

Key Takeaway: Politicization is the greatest enemy of reason facing the world today.

Presenting a variety of different psychological studies, Pinker shows us just how irrational we are, and how easily our political beliefs lead us to believe untrue statements that align with our existing thought. Confirmation bias is not a new concept—that we readily accept information that aligns with our beliefs and reject that which does not—but it's valuable to see it play out equally among both liberals and conservatives. Everyone is guilty of this and the more politically aligned you are, the stronger the effect.

In this, he provides an explanation for the support of wild conspiracy theories and patently untrue statements (such as that Obama was born in Kenya or Ted Cruz's father was in on the J.F.K. assassination) not as the stupidity of a particular person or group, but as a call to tribal belonging. Not believing that climate change is real, for example, has nothing to do with whether or not you've studied the science behind it, and everything to do with the fact that this belief is a prerequisite for membership in your particular party. Our beliefs are based more on this tribal belonging than on reason, which has led to politics looking more like rival football fans than an earnest discussion of what is best for a people and a nation.

Key Takeaway: For reason to prevail, we must depoliticize the conversation.

Both academia and the political media are subverting reason through increasingly politicized arguments and intolerance for opposing opinions. Pinker offers evidence that even those with strong political beliefs are able to address an argument with reason, so long as that argument isn't presented from a political standpoint. If you are liberal and an idea is presented by the left, you'll support it, by the right, and you won't, no matter the argument. But that same idea, presented as an objective suggestion by an unbiased party can lead to honest discourse and reasonable consensus between members of opposing teams.

Pinker admits that our understanding of biases may be too young to drive change any time soon, and we have many years to come of opposing pundits screaming repetitive talking points at one another on cable news. But the solution is there. The more we understand cognitive debiasing, the more we can apply it to our own thoughts and conversations every day. The more we teach students about critical thinking, checking sources, checking facts, and approaching an argument from both sides before making a decision, the better they will be at bringing that reasoning into adulthood.

CHAPTER 22

Science

Science is the greatest human accomplishment of all time. Unfortunately, many intellectuals view science as the enemy of elevated thought. Historians, philosophers, artists, and religious leaders consider science as mutually exclusive from, and inferior to, their disciplines. They are proponents of a theory known as "Second Culture" where science and the humanities operate independently from one another. They argue that the development of abstract thought, art, and philosophy is more important for humanity than any scientific discovery could be. This, of course, is patently false as science is responsible for all of the advancements that have cured disease and increased the quality of life in the past several centuries. Since academia is traditionally dominated by intellectuals in the humanities, the importance of science in education is downplayed and dismissed in many liberal arts universities.

Pinker argues strongly for the movement towards a "Third Culture" that would combine concepts from science and the humanities and apply them towards the humanistic goal of improving the lives of everyone around the world.

Key Takeaway: Science has been the scapegoat for many crimes against humanity throughout history.

Covering everything from Social Darwinism, eugenics, scientific racism, and the Holocaust, Pinker one-by-one debunks the pervasive myths that science was responsible for each of these atrocities. There is no discussion of genocide that is not culturally and morally based, and science as a discipline cannot be held responsible for the use of science to support a racist claim.

Key Takeaway: Science, religion, art, culture, history, philosophy, and morality are all inextricably intertwined.

While the intellectual left bashes science for its attempt to overtake culture and philosophy, and the religious right bashes science for its attempt to overtake morality and values, Pinker argues that neither is the case, and he is quick to impugn both sides. Science informs our understanding of all disciplines, and should be included, and is naturally a part of, any discussion thereof.

As much as scientists are not bound to discuss only matters of empirical fact, neither are philosophers forbidden from discussing matters of the physical world. Humanism, which informs the Enlightened morality of liberal democracies around the world, is based on scientific understanding and cannot be separated from it. Without science, we lose context for the rest of our advancement across other disciplines as well.

Key Takeaway: Liberal arts and the humanities need science in order to remain relevant in the Age of Information.

Much of Pinker's scathing commentary is directed at liberal arts colleges, where science is seen as the enemy of art, culture, and progress. Science has no place in a discussion of history or philosophy, which is leading professors, journalists, and politicians to fall prey to more cognitive biases, anecdotal arguments, and logical fallacies. A scientific mindset is useful no matter what discipline you're in and utilizing data (when we now have access to an unprecedented amount of it) is just as beneficial towards understanding whether or not UN Peacekeeping forces are effective as it is in testing the efficacy of a vaccine. Which, by the way, do NOT cause autism—another anti-science fervor induced by the far-left.

CHAPTER 23

Humanism

"Progress consists of deploying knowledge to allow all of humankind to flourish in the same way that each of us seeks to flourish" (Pinker, p. 410).

In the final chapter of the book, Pinker embarks on an epic exploration and defense of humanism, noting that when multiple nations of competing ideologies come together, they usually create something that aligns with humanistic ideals (such as the United Nations Declaration of Human Rights).

Before staging his grand defense against utilitarianism, theistic morality, fascism, authoritarian populism, and the philosophy of Nietzsche, Pinker reviews the key tenets of humanism as stated in *The Humanist Manifesto*, written in 2003 (pp. 410-411):

· Knowledge of the world is derived by observation, experimentation, and rational analysis.

· Humans are an integral part of nature, the result of unguided evolutionary change. . .

· Ethical values are derived from human need and interest as tested by experience.

· Life's fulfillment emerges from individual participation in the service of humane ideals.

· Humans are social by nature and find meaning in relationships.

· Working to benefit society maximizes individual happiness.

Key Takeaway: Humanism is the best basis for government, society, law, and morality that humans have come up with.

Pinker rattles through various arguments against humanism he has surely encountered time and again throughout his career, ticking off each and quickly refuting any rebuttals that may have popped into your head while contemplating the last point.

Theistic Morality

"If religion were a source of morality, the number of religious wars and atrocities ought to be zero" (Pinker, p. 430).

There are simply too many flaws in the argument for theistic morality: God (of any religion) hasn't provided enough of a moral basis to be reliable. Early stories in the Bible and the Quran alike advocate murder, slavery, and stoning the blasphemous—stories that supporters of both religions conveniently ignore.

While religion can be a source of love, compassion, charity, and generosity, in no way is it the only source of these ideals, and in no way has it contributed more to society than science, progress, and reason.

Authoritarianism, Populism, Reactionary Thinking, and Fascism

With the rise of these dangerous systems of rule, Pinker points out the one thinker who most fully embodies all of them: Nietzsche.

Nietzscheism is attractive to intellectuals and to authoritarian rulers because it expresses disdain for the common man, raises oneself above all others, and allows for a single, wiser, stronger, better person to implement their superior vision for the good of a society, as opposed to letting a society agree that what is good for you is good for me.

But the real danger in Nietzsche, and in turn populism and fascism, is the concept that one group or tribe is superior to another. It takes the evolution of a species and applies it to a specific sect, nation, or tribe in that species and calls for the literal extinction of all others. It is not hard to follow this thinking directly to the Holocaust.

And yet, populism tugs at the heart strings of those who feel marginalized, who feel their wealth, success, or way of life is being stolen. When societies experience broad increases in indicators of success and progress, they are more willing to move towards emancipative ideas. When the American middle class began to feel marginalized and left behind, their survival instincts kicked in, and their tribal mentality looked for anyone to blame.

The Case for Humanism

In closing, Pinker concedes that the world is not perfect, and it will never be. But the best chance we have to make it better is to continue to operate under the auspices of reason, humanism, science, and progress. We can continue to make the world better so long as we objectively and analytically test what is working and what is not, and we all agree:

"Life is better than death, health is better than sickness, abundance is better than want, freedom is better than coercion, happiness is better than suffering, and knowledge is better than superstition and ignorance" (Pinker, pp. 453-454).

EDITORIAL REVIEW

Enlightenment Now: The Case for Reason, Science, Humanism, and Progress is the *pièce de résistance* of Pinker's career. This epic tome of information utilizes the very ideals it espouses (reason and science) in order to drive home its main argument: that humanity is better off than ever before, and that we have Enlightenment-era ideals to thank for it.

Pinker's writing, though dense with statistics, remains accessible and entertaining throughout, and he is careful to never fall victim to his own biases. Every argument he makes is presented along with common counter arguments, their sources of information, and the sources he uses to refute them. There is not a single point made in the book without the data to back it up, and the data are convincing. The world does appear to be objectively better, by a long shot, no matter how many negative news stories we hear saying otherwise.

Despite his data-driven approach, however, the reader can't help but feel Pinker's optimism is a bit of a show. Each chapter feels like an exercise in saying, "See, I told you so!" and the possibility of cherry-picking data or interpreting data in a decidedly optimistic way remains open. For many counter-arguments Pinker presents, he quickly rejects them as untrue, despite the argument possibly deserving more than a dismissive refusal. Inequality, for example, is a real issue in the American economy and is causing massive amounts of distress on the lower middle class who—yes, still have more than they did twenty years ago—but that isn't so comforting when minimum wage is no longer livable, and CEOs are making more than 1,000 times the salary of their average employee. Dismissing this as "not really a problem since everyone is better off" doesn't really touch on the feeling of disenfranchisement so many Americans feel.

Similarly, in his discussion of happiness, he admits that Americans have not experienced the same across-the-board improvement that other countries have, but then attributes it to "women having more responsibility," "lower bars for diagnoses of mental disorders," or then justifies it by saying "anxiety is a sign of an Enlightened people who care." All of these arguments feel a bit like a cop-out, and maybe it's OK to say Americans feel more anxious because they are more anxious, and we're not exactly sure why this country is an anomaly to the rest of the Western world.

The data on safety, violence, health, and food production cannot be argued with and provide a refreshing perspective reminding us how much of our opinions are affected by biases both conscious and unconscious, and how much of what we see on the Internet and cable news can cloud our judgement of reality. If your own biases and logical fallacies aren't challenged by reading this book, you may need to take another look.

For all of Pinker's sunny optimism, the book ends on a much more realistic note. Pinker readily admits the forces working against the new Enlightenment, but makes a strong case for humanism as the best thing we as humans have come up with so far.

There is no one in the world who would not benefit from reading this book. Whether or not you ascribe to humanism as a belief system, the data alone are enough to give anyone additional perspective on the current state of the world. At the very least, this book relays with almost tedious specificity how far the world has come in the past few centuries, and what may lay on the road ahead.

BACKGROUND ON AUTHOR

Steven Arthur Pinker is a Canadian-American cognitive psychologist, linguist, and popular science author. He is one of the world's leading authorities on language and the mind, and he is a Professor of Psychology at Harvard University. *Enlightenment Now* is his eighth book.

Pinker's other titles have focused predominantly on visual cognition and psycholinguistics, arguing that the human faculty for language is an instinct. His sixth book, The *Better Angels of Our Nature*, is a precursor to *Enlightenment Now*, showcasing data that prove violence in societies has steadily declined over time.

Pinker was named one of *Time*'s most influential people in 2004, and in 2010 and 2011 he was named by Foreign Policy to its list of top global thinkers. He has received numerous awards for his work in cognitive psychology, and in May 2006 he received the American Humanist Association's Humanist of the Year award for his contributions to the public understanding of human evolution.

OTHER TITLES BY STEVEN PINKER

Language Learnability and Language Development (1984)

Visual Cognition (1985)

Connections and Symbols (1988)

Learnability and Cognition: The Acquisition of Argument Structure (1989)

Lexical and Conceptual Semantics (1992)

The Language Instinct (1994)

How the Mind Works (1997)

Words and Rules: The Ingredients of Language (1999)

The Blank Slate: The Modern Denial of Human Nature (2002)

The Stuff of Thought: Language as a Window into Human Nature (2007)

The Better Angels of Our Nature: Why Violence Has Declined (2011)

Language, Cognition, and Human Nature: Selected Articles (2013)

The Sense of Style: The Thinking Person's Guide to Writing in the 21st Century (September 30, 2014)

Enlightenment Now: The Case for Reason, Science, Humanism, and Progress (February 13, 2018)

END OF BOOK SUMMARY

If you enjoyed this *ZIP Reads* publication, we encourage you to purchase a copy of the original book from.

We'd also love an honest review on Amazon.com!

ZIP READS

19275158R00035

Made in the USA
Middletown, DE
04 December 2018